<u>I leave this for you</u>

<u>Part 1-7</u>

I leave this for you is a compilation of short selection of thoughts and poetry that I comprised of ideas and own experiences. based on personal moments and reflection of my life and times I sit and day dream. I pray you enjoy and get something out of it and also, I pray for your understanding.

<u>I leave this for you</u>

<u>Part 1</u>

Start by doing what's necessary then what's possible and suddenly you're doing the impossible.

<u>My Heart</u>

You keep me going you help me feel without feeling. I hurt so I understand I make you hurt. I've never seen you but you have seen me. You make me so brave but you also make me cry even when I don't want to. Giving me a feeling, I never felt before. I find it crazy that you break but are able to put yourself back together again. Been through the best of times and the worst of times. You fight for me every day and I know I be working you so much. I apologize for that and I thank you so much for that. Before you decide to give out on me, I promise to do my part to keep you going. I love you dearly........ my heart

Space love

My love for you is past the moon and the stars and galaxy. I crave for you every day and every night. You leave me breathless as if I'm in deep space no oxygen whatsoever. Leave me on a high where I'm never coming down back to earth. You are my world my new planet my ne embark on life. Nothing matters no one exist in our astral plane. Our love shines brighter than any star not even the sun comes close. Cool and full of light on a beautiful night with a full moon. I will forever be lost in space lost forever in your love.

<u>*Keep Going*</u>

As long as there is breath in me, I will fight no matter what type of issue is in my way. No matter how hard this life gets for me. I will walk with my head held high. It is so much more to life than what we can even imagine. Way much more than what is going on right now in this world. All praises all the time.

<u>Sometimes I just want to fly</u>

Sometimes I do but it's hard can't just up and leave. Not when people need you or depend on you, well some people anyway. My wings have been damaged over the years. Even when they are fixed and repaired, I still don't believe I can take flight. At this point I'm probably just scared of what the outcomes would be. But I guess its ok to imagine what the feeling may be. Even if I fly to outer space, I would still be met with different outcomes a whole new devil. Icarus flew too close to the sun and we know how that ended. Maybe that's why I say sometimes.

Time

Your oh so vast and so important I believe you came to present or of some sort. But then again you have me thinking in another order. Why do we as humans waste you. Everything about you counts bur I can't seem to keep up with you. They tell me you have healing powers but I still feel hurt and pain. Still losing track of you oh what a dangerous game. Everybody has you on their mind such a shame. Your ticking can literally drive a person insane. I definitely acknowledge your presence I do my best to stay sane. I can't take you for granted simple and plain.

You may encounter many defeats, but you must not be defeated. In fact, it may be necessary to encounter the defeats, so you can know who you are, what you can rise from, how you can still come out of it...... maya Angelou

Every night I stayed on it; I stayed focused kept grinding kept praying cause at the end of the day I knew I was going to be ok. I knew I was coming out of that dark place......... Roger Washington

<u>I leave this for you</u>

<u>Part 2</u>

<u>Save the children</u>

The most near perfect human beings walking this earth. We must protect them few seem to care and that is part of a serios problem. They are the future and they are so precious in every single way. Care for the kids guide them to the future for they are the future.

Pain

Pain is weakness leaving the body all mental in the mind. Trials and tribulations make you stronger. The heart hurts but fight it, keeping in mind that you are so much more. You are special you are chosen lock my body but can't trap my mind. It all some type of pain but it's just on different levels. I've been down before I do get better just stay true to yourself. Pain can't last forever keep your head up and push through it all.

Some more pain

I hurt I feel pain that I can't explain. I see that it is a bit of a problem I'm not good at playing a role. Being me is something I don't want to change or compromise. I lost well got rid of some pain but at the same time I gained more. I beat demons and new ones walked right up and my mind has been all over the place. Can't keep walking around blind to everything. I'm in need of help but don't really know where to look. Really don't understand why I even need it........ pain is not just physical

Time

Part 2

You can't waste time, well you can but definitely shouldn't. It does not take sides they say its everything but nothing at all. Patience hides behind especially when you're trying to make a change in your life. And never forget that it waits for no man at all. Do you really know how much time you have for anything?

*I feel so out of touch growing further from my people.

*Don't let things that don't matter effect you.

*Everything happens for a reason be grateful for the reason whatever it may be.

*Love everything and everyone the Most High is love.

Matthew 19:26

But Jesus beheld thee and said to them with men this is impossible but with God all things are possible.

I leave this for you

Part 3

There is nothing noble in being superior to your fellow man. True nobility is being superior to your former self……. Ernest Hemingway

Time

Part 3

Stop hitting the snooze button we don't have much left. We may think we might, sounds funny but time operates on its own timing. Crazy we have these time zones but in reality, nobody can guard it it changes when it feels like or gets ready too. We move and make our life choices around it. No wonder why they say I wish there were more hours in a day. I wish I could turn back the hands of time truly. Slow down I really need more time of you and I know you know it. I get tired of trying to figure out how to manage you better. I just need more of you is all im trying to say. Why do you have to be so important to me and so many others as well ……. time

<u>Rain</u> (The Good)

You are just different extraterrestrial in a sense out of this world really. Well at least the atmosphere you have an important job. This earth really needs you and love you. Most people dislike when you come around but for me it's cool. I understand you are needed not all the time but yes you are needed. Somehow you find a way to calm my nerves and settle my mood. On a few occasions you have tucked me in for bed some of my best sleep I must say. You have your ways and your moods coming down pretty bad on all of us sometimes. But in other ways you sprinkle lightly and then disappear. I've seen the sun shine so bright and you still find a way to show up with a beautiful rainbow. I promise you can make a hot day so cool almost instantly. You are here forever not every day but I can guarantee you will be on your way...

Breathe

I know some people find it hard to do and in reality, its beyond easy. I mean we do it unconditionally, uncontrollably. But I understand I mean the pressure the weight of this world hits randomly or surprisingly. It comes and puts all that pressure on your chest where in turn you're fighting for air. Getting ready to panic if not already at that point. But please just stop and breathe you have to you have no choice. A lot of people don't think they do but that choice is yours. You have to believe you have to know everything is going to be ok. I know it's hard sometimes you can't even think straight or focus when certain real-life things hit us. But this thing called breathing we do it every day and every minute. Through our nose our mouths we do it in our sleep it's just in us to do so. So, tell me why when a problem comes in to effect, we can't just stop and breathe.

<u>Rain</u> *(The Bad)*

Rain rain go away come again another day, sometimes you love to overstay your welcome. And as much as I like you and you cover me you can be just as bad for me. You can definitely make that known you have stayed so long I couldn't get anything done. You seem to trap me in the house all day at times when I want to leave. Don't let it get cold and lonely that's when depression starts to take over. I hate the feeling because I be thinking that you are never going to let up. Sometime you even start coming down so hard I just be wishing you could go away. Making so much of a mess for me and everyone else having us reschedule and make new plans. Just let us miss you some times.

Most of the important things in the world have been accomplished by people who have kept on trying when there seemed to be no hope at all......... Dale Carnegie

I leave this for you

Part 4

Save the children

Part 2

Bless, they heart I love and care for you all I wish more people would see you as I do. They need help they need love they need better guidance. Then what we they are receiving now. Most High bless these children for they are the future. Bless us as adults to be better for these kids are much so lost. These kids are committing crimes they are killing each other and have no respect for the elderly. They seem to be brainwashed and programmed in a way past repair. Is this what our future is, do we really want to call them or even rely on them for the future? There's no way that looks good for us and I believe it's never too late to change. Their perspective on life is so important we have to fix it. I have faith we can save the children, as Marvin Gaye once sung about. Its starts with you as a person we as people. That one rock thrown in the ocean can be a change it will set off that ripple effect. A big problem is that we are doing nothing to change their lives. I encourage us as people to do something anything say something. If we get off our phones maybe they will get off theirs you are the reflection. I pray for your understanding.

From whom the bells toll

That feeling when the world has pinned you down in a place that you didn't even know existed. That place where your world doesn't exist anymore. Things you though you knew look unfamiliar. You are trying your best to shake back but something won't let you so you fold. Seems like no matter what you try you fail miserably stuff around you just grows darker. Lonely all to yourself and you're searching for any light any spark and can't even seem to find it. Everyone sees this and knows that you are hurting. But it's so heavy they don't do nothing to save you or help they probably can't even if they wanted to. They hear your cries and screams but are they really listing? The thoughts in your head become vicious and lethal you are past the point of questioning is this real? Is this even me talking like this? The fight or whatever fight you thought you was putting up is to no success. I don't lose hope my faith is very strong but this time it's gone like it was never here. There's nothing, I can do my mind is too far gone for any self-saving. Not in the right place to even ask for the right help. Thank you Most High for having mercy and saving me that day. I was him whom which the bells tolled.

<u>Karma</u>

<u>Part 1</u>

The day I met you I still couldn't believe you are beaty in a sense. I say this because justice will always prevail in the end. If I do anything you are waiting in the wind on the perfect time for your big reveal. Can't help myself sometimes I guess it's free will. I can really count on you to always come back and seal the deal. I guess fate it is as you would have it. It didn't take me much time to know that you are real and sometimes so shocking as an electric eel. Sorry, that saying never gets old to me inside joke. I know you will always be around so I guess I'll be seeing you soon.........., Karma

I was never really insane except upon the occasions when my heart was truly touched......... Edgar Allen Poe

I leave this for you

Part 5

Those who dream by day are cognizant of many things which escape those who dream only by night............ Edgar Allen Poe

The Madness

Do you see it, it's everywhere all around us, the feeling is off the vibe isn't right. Can you smell it a stench of death so strong and we can't even sniff it out. Disguised in so much perfume to seem pretty. Why is it so easy to ignore? Why do I feel like I'm the only one who notices this? This world is so uncivilized its right in our faces. Wonder why they call this life a race. It's because it is a race in fact, a race against ourselves a race against time. And they made you believe that you weren't even racing. It's not a specific thing man to be fair I don't even know what to call it. I just know it's a real problem it's not of love or of care. It's just not right and it's so off tome. As I watch the blind leading the blind, I will just call it the madness....

Karma

Part 2

I knew you would be back to see about some decisions I made. To be honest I'm not even mad see I'm starting to figure you out. You really mean no harm at all and really you are just doing your intended purpose. I see that you don't like to be rubbed the wrong way and I can definitely understand that. You also have a problem with people lying to you, I find that you don't really like that at all. You just want people to be good to each other love other. Which in reality is not asking for much because all you plan on doing is returning the favor or good deeds sown. I will focus and make sure I keep sowing these great seeds of good. I know I will see it come back in the future. I know that you make good on your promises, so in a weird way I'm starting to like you. I see you for who you really are I will see you around my friend....... Karma

<u>My Heart</u>

<u>Part 2</u>

I thank you for doing better at making me treat you a lot better. I know your still hurting at times but not as much now days so that's good. You're getting stronger I can tell by how I'm treating you. Making better decisions in life I know you are going to last a lot longer. I'm more focused on putting less pressure and strain on you. I see all you really need is love and that's all you are trying to give. So, I will do my part on those things. Funny how that kind of stuff makes you feel. You do have a mind of your own truly that I have to respect. I have no quarrel with that at all. The sound your beat is very different nowadays, I'm very grateful for that. If there is anything else whatever it is to make you feel better at the end of the day, I'm all for it. I love you you are my heart literally............ I pray for your understanding

Suffering has been stronger than all other life teachings, and has taught me to understand what your heart used to be. I've been bent and broken, but I hope into better shape ….Charles Dickens

<u>*Proverbs 27:19*</u>

As water reflects the face, so one's life reflects the heart….

<u>I leave this for you</u>

<u>Part 6</u>

<u>Self-discipline</u>

I so need you right now I miss you a lot. I remember when it was in basic training for the U.S Army, you were forced upon me to have you is a blessing. It changed my life all around I need you back in my life. Having you can make things boring in a sense due to the struggle. But with you things can be great I know this from experience. You kept me out of a lot of trouble you made me a different person a higher quality of myself. You fixed my health the positive effects that you can bring cane be endless. Whatever a person can be dealing with in life or going through, with self-discipline you can overcome anything. Whether it be a drinking issue a bad smoking habit cheating or a gambling problem. These addictions are very possible to beat the can all be fixed. All it takes is some good old fashion self-discipline yes, it's tough but I promise at the end of the day the results are amazing. What type of life do you really want to live?

Karma

Part 3

Here we are beautiful and things are much better than our last meeting. I'm in a better place with you I believe we are good friends now. The things you have presented to you of lately have been in good spirits. I'm at peace when you come my way now and that's wonderful. You are a law of this world and I pray more people understand that and come to respect that. They have to treat you better, or at least see you differently as I do. If everyone in this world would greet you with love and good intentions. Man, this world would be a beautiful place I see you working in it a lot of people are starting to wake up and realize your power. I think it's because they are tired of you coming back, the way with bad news. And they will know that they don't like seeing you like that. If you know better than you have to do better at some point everyone is responsible for their actions. Love you Karma I know what our bond looks like so let's keep this great thing going.

<u>Galatians 6 7:9</u>

7 Do not be deceived; God cannot be mocked. A man reaps what he sows. 8 The one who sows to please his sinful nature, from that nature will reap destruction; the one who sows to please the spirit will reap eternal life. 9 Let us not become weary in doing good for at the proper time we will reap a harvest if don't give up.

I leave this for you

Part 7

The Sun

I see you up there so high in the sky shining o so bright. I just want to tell you thank you for doing so. You bring so much life to the lifeless and so many other things. If no one has told you so I will, thank you so beautiful and bright I pray your light never goes out. I still wonder why my father calls me sunny I mean I kind of know but I feel like it's much more to it just as it is to you. On a bad day you can hit at the right time and have me wondering why I was even mad in the first place. Love to see you come check on me after a tough rainy day. You been around forever and I hope it stays that's way so others can see such a bright beauty.

The Moon

Just like your other half I do so enjoy you equally also. When you are all fat and full it is a beautiful sight. Your glow is un denying such a marvel to see. At times I just stare and get lost in you, it can get spooky at times but still you are suck a pretty sight. You give so much light to the darkness so I know you mean well. Posted up there with your entourage the stars you sure know how to put on a show in the night sky. Very mysterious how you change your shape up like that. Personally, I think the crescent is kind of cool if I may say. Crazy how I've seen you change colors and scientist still are finding new things about you but honestly, I could care less what they say. I'm just going to enjoy you enjoy the shows you put on. I do have one request I hope you bring out your friends out a lot more, you know them stars they really be doing they thing. Love you I'll be waiting to see you again tonight, don't keep me waiting now I'll be looking up later on for you.

The Ocean

Beautiful you are so much of on this planet of ours is crazy. I don't have to put the numbers on here everybody just about knows but you are something to sea. Get it sea no, but seriously the mysteries of you are wild you haven't even been fully explored. Which I do find so baffling still to this day. Holding so much life you are very vast I can just sit and catch a great vibe from looking at you. So smooth so chill and still just a really great fell. You can be so soft and gentle the way your waves move. But at the same time, you can be devasting and destructive crashing hard into things. You have a color of your own that ocean blues o man and when the sun hits and give that sparkle shine. And then the sun be trying to hide behind makes that date that much better. Yall make the perfect pair with that one. When I sit my feet in you something happens that I kind of just can't explain I just know it's something special. You still give me a small fear factor of your unknowing depts. But still such a great wonder the Most High has blessed us with.

Genesis 1:16

And God made the two great lights the greater to rule the day and the lesser to rule the night and stars.

Genesis 1:5-7

5 God called the light day and the darkness night and there was evening and there was morning the first day. 6 And God said let there be an expanse between the waters to separate water from water. 7 So God made the expanse and separated the water under the expanse from the water above.